Letters to You

The Complete Collection

Lena Ma

Contents

Letters to the Forgotten:

Prologue	3
Letters to you	7
Chapter 1	9
Write down all the words that are running	13
Draw an image that represents how you are feeling this very moment.	15
Chapter 2	16
Write down all the words that are running	19
Draw an image that represents how you are feeling this very moment.	21
Chapter 3	22
Write down all the words that are running	27
Draw an image that represents how you are feeling this very moment.	29
Chapter 4	30
Write down all the words that are running	35
Draw an image that represents how you are feeling this very moment.	37
Chapter 5	38
Write down all the words that are running	43
Draw an image that represents how you are feeling this very moment.	45
Chapter 6	46
Write down all the words that are running	51
Draw an image that represents how you are feeling this very moment.	53
Chapter 7	54
Write down all the words that are running	59

Draw an image that represents how you are feeling this very moment.	61
Chapter 8	62
Write down all the words that are running	67
Draw an image that represents how you are feeling this very moment.	69
Chapter 9	70
Write down all the words that are running	73
Draw an image that represents how you are feeling this very moment.	75
Chapter 10	76
Write down all the words that are running	81
Draw an image that represents how you are feeling this very moment.	83
Letters To Me	85
A Letter To Those Fighting To Survive:	87
A Letter To Those Who Struggle To Forgive Themselves:	89
A Letter To Those Who Have Been Rejected:	91
A Letter To Those Who Do Not Believe In Themselves:	93
A Letter To Those Who Find It Difficult To Speak Up:	95
A Letter To Those Who Need A Supportive Hand:	97
Epilogue	98
Reminder To Love Everyone	101

Letters to Those Loved & Lost:

MAD GIRL'S LOVE SONG	107
Prologue	109
Chapter 1	113
Write a letter expressing your true feelings to your first crush.	117

Draw an image representing the agony of how you feel around your first crush.	119
Chapter 2	120
Write a letter expressing your true feelings to your first crush.	123
Draw an image representing the agony of how you feel around your first crush.	125
Chapter 3	126
Write a letter expressing your true feelings to your first crush.	129
Draw an image representing the agony of how you feel around your first crush.	131
Chapter 4	132
Write a letter expressing your true feelings to your first crush.	135
Draw an image representing the agony of how you feel around your first crush.	137
Chapter 5	138
Write a letter expressing your true feelings to your first crush.	141
Draw an image representing the agony of how you feel around your first crush.	143
Chapter 6	144
Write a letter expressing your true feelings to your first crush.	147
Draw an image representing the agony of how you feel around your first crush.	149
Chapter 7	150
Write a letter expressing your true feelings to your first crush.	155
Draw an image representing the agony of how you feel around your first crush.	157
Chapter 8	158
Write a letter expressing your true feelings to your first crush.	161
Draw an image representing the agony of how you feel around your first crush.	163

Chapter 9	164
Write a letter expressing your true feelings to your first crush.	169
Draw an image representing the agony of how you feel around your first crush.	171
Chapter 10	172
Write a letter expressing your true feelings to your first crush.	177
Draw an image representing the agony of how you feel around your first crush.	179
Chapter 11	180
Write a letter expressing your true feelings to your first crush.	183
Draw an image representing the agony of how you feel around your first crush.	185
Chapter 12	186
Write a letter expressing your true feelings to your first crush.	189
Draw an image representing the agony of how you feel around your first crush.	191
Chapter 13	192
Write a letter expressing your true feelings to your first crush.	195
Draw an image representing the agony of how you feel around your first crush.	197
Chapter 14	198
Write a letter expressing your true feelings to your first crush.	201
Draw an image representing the agony of how you feel around your first crush.	203
Chapter 15	204
Write a letter expressing your true feelings to your first crush.	207
Draw an image representing the agony of how you feel around your first crush.	209
Chapter 16	210

Write a letter expressing your true feelings to your first crush.	215
Draw an image representing the agony of how you feel around your first crush.	217
Chapter 17	218
Write a letter expressing your true feelings to your first crush.	221
Draw an image representing the agony of how you feel around your first crush.	223
Chapter 18	224
Write a letter expressing your true feelings to your first crush.	227
Draw an image representing the agony of how you feel around your first crush.	229
Chapter 19	230
Write a letter expressing your true feelings to your first crush.	235
Draw an image representing the agony of how you feel around your first crush.	237
Chapter 20	238
Write a letter expressing your true feelings to your first crush.	241
Draw an image representing the agony of how you feel around your first crush.	243
Epilogue	244
Love Letter	247
Acknowledgments	249

The Passion Of My Desolation

1. The Blade Of My Right Hand	255
2. My Heart, I Surrender	258
3. Terminal Faith	260
4. My Last Journey, Forever	262
5. Without You, I Feel Nothing	264
6. Blood Seeps In My Silent Battle	267

7.	A Robotic Slave	271
8.	Chasing Wind	273
9.	Survival Of Endless Nights	276
10.	Lady Misfortune	279
11.	Nothing But Scars Left Behind	281
12.	Stabbing Shadows From My Past	283
13.	Individuality Behind The Mask	285
14.	Tragedy That Is My Existence	287
15.	Trapped Inside My Treacherous Body	289
16.	Lust In My Champagne	291

Letters to You:
The Complete Collection
Lena Ma

Copyright © 2020

All rights reserved. No part of this publication may be reproduced, distributed, or transmitted in any form or by any means, including photocopying, recording, or other electronic or mechanical methods, without the prior written permission of the publisher, except in the case of brief quotations embodied in critical reviews and certain other noncommercial uses permitted by copyright law.

Any references to historical events, real people, or real places are used fictitiously. Names, characters, and places are products of the author's imagination.

Cover Design by EmCat Designs

Letters to the Forgotten:

Your Struggles Do Not Define You

Prologue

We all know the saying, "Never judge a book by its cover." Sadly, few of us follow this mantra, and we judge everyone and
everything without an attempt to know and understand them.
We have all been victims and perpetrators of hate, criticism, and ugliness.

Lena Ma

We have all opened our mouths seconds too soon and have forgotten that we are human, just like everyone else, struggling to survive in this world.
Life is difficult enough without the
harsh words of our peers.

We fight instead of love.
We push away instead of understand.
We falsely believe that we are superior to others because of our looks, our status, our upbringings, or just our grandiose mentalities.

We often forget how, without the help of those we criticize, our society would not stand the way it does today, even if it is not apparent at the time.

We forget that, as much as we push people away, it is the same people we push away that want to understand us the most.
But we are scared.
We are scared to lose the mask we so meticulously crafted for ourselves.

Letters to the Forgotten:

We are scared to become vulnerable because we have been hurt before.
We are scared to trust anyone but ourselves because we believe they will never understand us.
We all believe we are unique, with our own unique problems and struggles, and sharing these problems will cause everyone to despise us and look down on us.

Our problems are not unique, nor are they so different and far-fetched from everyone else's that we need to shelter them from the world.
Let's not forget that we are all the same.
We are all part of one family who struggle to fit in, and we just want to be loved.
We are all beautiful human beings despite the many actions and/or words we express to prove to ourselves and others otherwise.

We are not beautiful based on the standard norms of beauty.
Beauty comes from our hearts.
If we feel beautiful, then we are, despite hateful words of others.
Never let anyone else tell you or make you feel ugly and worthless because you create your own beauty.

These letters were written from my heart to yours

Lena Ma

because we all need to be reminded that we are all special, even when life tells us that we are not.

These letters serve as constant reminders for all of us to love and accept ourselves, even during times when no one else does.

Letters to you

Chapter One

A Letter To Those Overwhelmed By Anxiety: We Are All Warriors

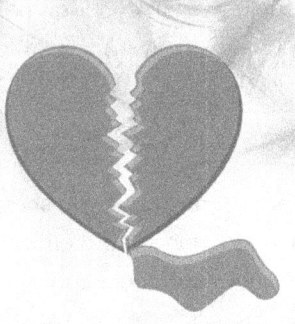

Imagine getting on a plane and completely forgetting whether you turned your stove off.
How do you feel?
Now imagine experiencing that feeling every minute of every day.
That is what anxiety feels like.

Lena Ma

Anxiety is being in a state of constant worry and not being able to turn it off.
But anxiety is not a disorder.
Anxiety is not a flaw.
Anxiety is a survival technique and protection mechanism designed to help you get through life.

While everyone else is blindly jumping into the hole,
you are
processing what is in that hole, and the consequences you will face if you also jump.
Anxiety is a creative process inside your head that helps you sort through to the best plan of action before diving in head first.

Anxiety is not a fault you should hide.
Instead, it is a strength you should embrace because it helps make you stronger and more courageous to face the monsters in this world.

People will tell you that it is crippling to live with constant worry inside your head because you never get the chance to relax.
But you do relax.
You are smart enough to know that once you figure out the best plan of action, you can sit back in peace, knowing that you have made the right decision.

Letters to the Forgotten:

Anxiety does not make you flawed.
Anxiety makes you a warrior because you are able to turn clutter into blueprints in order to survive.
Being on your toes all the time helps you get through life in one piece.
There are days where you may want to give up, days where you may want to just make an impulsive decision and move on, worry-free.

I get it.
Being worried all the time is time-consuming, and it is extremely difficult when you feel like everyone else is moving forward except you.
But the truth is, they are not moving forward.

We are all moving at our own pace, and those who seem to be moving forward, can also move back.
No one knows the exact path that they are going to take.
This is just your path, and that is okay.
Accept that you are living a creative process and love yourself for that.
It is an amazing place to be because you are turning fire into flame, and that is a skill to be proud of.

Write down all the words that are running

Through your head this very moment. Do not think. Just write.

Draw an image that represents how you are feeling this very moment.

Do not think. Just draw.

Chapter Two

A Letter To Those Feeling Lost And Alone: You Matter, And You Will Be Found

Do you feel lost?
Do you feel like the world around you is moving on while you remain stagnant and stuck?

Letters to the Forgotten:

Do you feel as if no one will notice if you suddenly disappeared into the darkness?
You feel alone.

You feel unaccomplished.
You feel invisible and simply trudging through life, one monotonous step at a time.
But this is just a feeling.

Everyone, even the most "successful", at one time, has also experienced this feeling.
Remember, feelings are not reality, and "feeling lost" is not "being lost".

You are present, you are here, and you matter in this world.
You may not think that people around you see you, but they do.
If you are gone, they will notice an absence.

You feel that they do not notice you now because they know that you are always there, that you are reliable and loyal.
This feeling will fade.
Although it seems never-ending, someone will come along and find you again.
It may be another person or it may be you.

Lena Ma

Someone will help you find light again and show you how this world, and the lives of people around you, will completely change if you are gone.
You don't have to feel like you have purpose now because you are purpose.

Being alive means you are already found.
You may not notice, but people see you.
When you look in the mirror, you see you.
That's all the evidence that you need.
So just keep breathing.

Stop trying so hard to be seen because your presence is already radiant.
Accept that you are simply experiencing a feeling, and that reality is much more different.

More importantly, if you are ever feeling alone, remember that someone else in this world is also feeling the same.
And if you can find a reason to feel hope again, maybe they can too.

Be the change for yourself and for others.

Write down all the words that are running

Through your head this very moment. Do not think. Just write.

Draw an image that represents how you are feeling this very moment.

Do not think. Just Draw.

Chapter Three

**A Letter To Those Fighting A Battle Within:
You Are Stronger Than You Think**

The greatest battle we will ever fight is the battle within ourselves.
The greatest enemy we will ever have is our own

Letters to the Forgotten:

conscience.
The greatest compassion we will ever feel is our own self-acceptance.

Every day, we are in a constant battle with ourselves, whether it involves how we look, how we behave, words that do or do not come out of our mouths, how we love, who we love, what we become, who we become, etc.

Our heads become convoluted with back and forth nonsense about how we are not good enough.
Isn't it enough that we already fight the hate and judgments of others?
Why make life that much more difficult by adding onto the war?

We are the most intelligent yet the most vulnerable.
We know who we are and who we want to be but doubt ourselves every step of the way.

We constantly compare ourselves to others in how we are not pretty enough, not smart enough, not rich enough, or not successful enough, and in return, we completely ignore the gifts that we do have.
We are pretty enough.

Lena Ma

We are smart enough.
We are rich enough, and we are successful enough.
What we are not, however, is confident enough.

Even if we try to tell ourselves every day that we are good and worthy, we still let the influences of others change our minds.
But let's give self-doubt, external hate, and internal battles the finger, and walk away with pride, proud of who we already are and confident enough to stand by ourselves when no one else will.
We may be our greatest enemies, but we are also our greatest allies, and by learning to stop fighting our internal battles and accepting parts of us we believe are flaws, we are relieved from our worst heartaches.
Every one of us is born different.

When we try to be like everyone else, we lose the qualities that make us unique and different.
When we try so hard to fit in, we become lost, and we lose our individualities.
Our doubt and self-hatred are strong, polluted by the society around us.
I get it.

Letters to the Forgotten:

However, I also believe that we all have the strength to overcome anything, and the moment we can conquer our sins against ourselves, that is the moment we can declare victory against life's war.

Write down all the words that are running

Through your head this very moment. Do not think. Just write.

Draw an image that represents how you are feeling this very moment.

Do not think. Just draw.

Chapter Four

**A Letter To Those Dealing With Toxic People:
It's Okay To Leave;
You Do Not Owe Them Your Life**

We all have those people in our lives, the ones who only

Letters to the Forgotten:

contribute stress, negativity, and misery without the benefit of anything positive.
These people can be our families, our friends, our partners, or our colleagues.
These are the people who know we care and take advantage of us.
These are the people who will screw us over every chance they get because they know we will always be there.
These are the charmers, the ones with the face of an angel but the heart of the devil.
These are the people we need to walk away from.

I recently lost a friend who would constantly cut me out of his life for simply having an opinion and not catering to his every need.
I recently lost a partner who, no matter what I did, would always leave, knowing I would take him back whenever he saw convenient.

Losing someone is never easy, despite how terribly they behaved.
We invest so much time and energy into people that we feel guilty if we leave and betrayed if they leave.

But what happens when we stay?
What happens when we let toxic people walk all over us,

forgiving them unconditionally while all they do is bring us pain?
We end up losing our own lives and our own happiness to protect that of others.

It is time we finally put our feet down and walk away from those who only bring us heartache.
It is time we stop feeling guilty for living for our own happiness.
We can still love toxic people, but we also need to learn when to walk away before we completely lose our voice and our freedom.

We need to stand up against those who treat us poorly, and more times than not, walking away from them is the best way to do so.
Don't ever feel guilty for taking back your own life, especially when the other person doesn't feel guilty for stealing it.

When you start surrounding yourself with positive people who only want the best for you, you start realizing that you have choices and a mind of your own.
Unconditionally loving someone who doesn't love you back only shows that you have a heart that should be shared with those who will also share their hearts with you.

Letters to the Forgotten:

Do not regret having shared your life with a toxic person. Loving someone who hurt you is a beautiful gift and an incredible feat of selflessness.

Write down all the words that are running

Through your head this very moment. Do not think. Just write.

Draw an image that represents how you are feeling this very moment.

Do not think. Just draw.

Chapter Five

**A Letter To Those Dealing With A Broken Heart:
You Deserve Better**

We have all been there.
A broken heart, crushed by someone we once loved and trusted.

Letters to the Forgotten:

Whether it is a short-term breakup or a long-term divorce, a broken heart is a broken heart, and it leaves us feeling like we just want to die.

But it will get better, I promise!
It may not feel like it in the moment, but think of all the other times you have dealt with the same feeling, and with time, the pain has lessened, right?

I know you're thinking that this time isn't the same as the other times, or this person meant so much more than the ones in the past.
I know the feeling.
I have been there, and trust me, things were not pretty for me either.

Even if you do not believe that it will get better, believe that you deserve to be loved and cared for by someone who doesn't walk out on you or betray you when life becomes difficult.
Believe that one day, someone will come along and give you the world rather than vice versa.
Believe that you will find someone, where no matter what you say or do, that person will still love you regardless because they see and love you as a person, not for your actions or status.

Believe that, even though you may never forget the current person, you will replace this face with a new one.
Believe that you are worth so much more than the betrayals of someone who hurt you.
So often we still settle for people who may not be the best for us.

We see arguments and unfaithfulness as a commonality rather than a problem, and we ignore our brains telling us that there is someone better out there because we are so afraid of ending up alone.

We settle for relationships where the other person does not love us, but instead only tolerates us enough to stick around, because we lie to ourselves that this is the best we can do.
But you know it isn't!
Even if you may not see it, I see it!

I see that we are all beautiful and kind-hearted people who deserve to be treated with the same love and compassion we give others.
We deserve so much more than someone who can only love us conditionally.
I promise that the right person will come around.
Patience and self-respect are keys to all happiness.

Letters to the Forgotten:

The more love we show ourselves, the more love others can begin to show us.
The radiance that comes from within us captures the radiance that we crave from those around us.

Write down all the words that are running

Through your head this very moment. Do not think. Just write.

Draw an image that represents how you are feeling this very moment.

Do not think. Just draw.

Chapter Six

**A Letter To Those Who Feel Like Their Life Is Falling Apart:
It Is, But You Don't Have To**

Everything and everyone around you are either falling apart or destroying themselves.

Letters to the Forgotten:

I get it.
Every minute of the day, you feel like you want to close your eyes for the final time.
Every agony you face, you feel like you would rather die.
I get it.
Your life is slowly crumbling into pieces, and you are tired of trying to hold it together, just to watch it fall apart again.

Some days you walk past a bridge and wonder, even for a second, how all your problems can finally be over if you just jumped.
I get it.
But I need to tell you that running away or shutting yourself out to avoid situations in which you cannot fix is not the answer.

As painstakingly debilitating as having to deal with problems is, it only helps build you stronger.
Just because moments around you are hell, does not mean you also have to live in hell.

Life will always suck, and you will always feel like you want to end it all rather than face it.
If not this one, it will be the next.
You will even face moments that will rip your soul out and make you wish you were never born.

Lena Ma

But when that moment comes, you will be ready.
For you have already claimed victory over your other battles in life.
You will be strong enough to win the war because you have not given up.

Are you still with me?
Good.

During this next minute, don't do anything else besides read what is on this page.
You have come too far to give up now.
You have fought and won many battles already.
If you stop now, all your achievements would have been for nothing.

You are strong enough to get through whatever it is you are facing because you have done it many times before.

You believe you are not strong enough now, but you are just scared.
I am also terrified.
But where there is fear, there is also courage.

Letters to the Forgotten:

I need you to keep living.
If you can't do it for yourself, do it for me.

I need you to keep fighting so I can also keep fighting.
Let us both come down from the ledge and defeat life together, okay?
I will always be here with you.

Here, take my hand.
Let's go.

Write down all the words that are running

Through your head this very moment. Do not think. Just write.

Draw an image that represents how you are feeling this very moment.
Do not think. Just draw.

Chapter Seven

**A Letter To Those Struggling With Acceptance:
Begin By Learning To Accept Yourself**

You crave acceptance.
We all do.
You change your hair, your clothes, even your personality,
in attempts to gain acceptance.

Letters to the Forgotten:

You want those around you, peers and strangers alike, to simply like you and accept you for who you already are.
But they do not.
And it drives you insane.

You continue changing.
You spend hours researching the most likeable personality traits you can possess, and you spend your life-savings on transient lifestyles that you believe will give you an edge, despite your feelings toward them.

You keep trying.
Trying until your body gives out and your brain overloads.
You give until you have nothing left to give except for blood and bones.

Nothing changes.
They still do not accept you.
You still feel like you are on the outside.
No matter what you do, they will never let you in.

You cry.
You want this to end.

Lena Ma

You want to stop feeling like you have nothing left.
You just want acceptance.

But you cannot obtain it the one way you have been trying.
So, what do you do?
You try again.
In a different way.
Rather than looking toward your surroundings, you look within.
Rather than seeking acceptance from your peers and strangers, you seek acceptance from yourself.

You cannot control whether others accept or reject you.
But you can control whether you accept or reject yourself.
Right now, you have been rejecting yourself.
Seeking fulfillment from others because that is what you have been taught to do.

Place your hand over the left side of your chest.
Do you feel that?
Do you feel that rhythmic beating?
That is the melody to your unique life.
From the loving and accepting heart that you possess.

Feel your heart.

Letters to the Forgotten:

Use it.
Remind yourself that you also possess a heart capable of acceptance.
When others fail to see the beauty that you are, place your hand over your chest and remember that you can see your own beauty.

When you crave acceptance from others, remind yourself that you do not have to destroy yourself for it.
You can give acceptance to yourself, and that is all that you need.

Write down all the words that are running

Through your head this very moment. Do not think. Just write.

Draw an image that represents how you are feeling this very moment.

Do not think. Just draw.

Chapter Eight

**A Letter To Those Feeling Pressured To Succeed:
Societal Standards Are Only Optional;
You Can Create Your Own Rules**

Letters to the Forgotten:

From the day you were born, what were you told?
Attend the top universities, climb the career ladder, and settle down with a loving family.
You listen with a smile because you have not learned any other way.

A decade down the road, you realize that life is not the fairytale story you were told as a child.
Life is much more difficult and complicated.

Life gives you the ingredients and options to live that fairytale story, but life also gives you unexpected results.
You continue your journey toward what you were told: education, career, and family.
But that smile is no longer there.

You feel empty.
You tell yourself that you are the only one not succeeding, while everyone else is.

You begin to wonder whether there is something wrong with you, why you are not able to match up to your peers.
Are they simply better at living life?
You look down in despair, unable to pull your head out of your own personal misery.

Lena Ma

But then you feel the wind.
You look up.
You look around.
You see everyone robotically moving in the same direction that you were told.
But none of them are smiling.
Even when they are surrounded by diplomas and paychecks.

You question yourself again.
Why is no one smiling if they are living life the way they should be?

Maybe I am not alone.
Maybe no one has this figured out.
Maybe reality is not a fairytale after all.

If everyone around me is living life the way they were told and are still not happy, maybe happiness comes from living outside the boundaries.

Maybe I can create my own happiness by living the life I choose rather than the life chosen for me.

Letters to the Forgotten:

Maybe I can finally break out of what society has ingrained into my brain and change the way that life should be lived.
Maybe I can learn to smile again.
Just maybe.

Write down all the words that are running

Through your head this very moment. Do not think. Just write.

Draw an image that represents how you are feeling this very moment.

Do not think. Just draw.

Chapter Nine

**A Letter To Those Overwhelmed With Stress
And Frustration:
Breathe**

I know you have those moments.

Letters to the Forgotten:

Moments where the entire world just seems to aggravate you.
Moments where you wish you could punch a hole through a wall and unleash all the anger you have pent up inside of you.
Moments where you simply want to be isolated and alone, forever.

Those moments are real.
We have all struggled with those moments.
The moments where we have not been triggered, but the frustration is still there.

You want it to stop.
You hate lashing out at anyone who tries to speak to you because it is not fair to them.
They have done nothing wrong.
Yet, you still unleash.

You feel as if your head is about to explode.
You want it to all go away.
You try distractions.
You try self-medicating.
You even try isolation.
But nothing seems to work.

Lena Ma

You just want to stop thinking.
I know.
Just breathe.
Breathe in.
And out.
In.

And out.
In.
Out.
Breathe.
Breathe.
Breathe.

Write down all the words that are running

Through your head this very moment. Do not think. Just write.

Draw an image that represents how you are feeling this very moment.

Do not think. Just draw.

Chapter Ten

**A Letter To Those Searching For Self-Love:
You Already Have It**

You feel sad.
You visit a psychologist.
She spends an hour explaining what you already know.

Letters to the Forgotten:

You leave.
Feeling unfulfilled.
Still sad.
You visit a psychiatrist.
He writes up a prescription in a blink of an eye and sends you on your way.

You take the drug.
Wait 3 days.
Still sad.
But now with an empty wallet.

You sit on the curb.
Confused.
Drugs in one hand.
Knife in the other.
You are tired of being your own worst enemy.

You want it to stop.
You do your research.
20 self-help books.
30 self-love blogs.
Nothing.

You still feel sad.

Lena Ma

You lie in bed, unable to sleep, wondering why you even exist.
You stay silent.
Tears drip down your cheeks.
Silence.
Quiet.

But then you hear something.
A brisk and mellow gust of wind.
It goes away.
Silence.
Quiet.

You hear it again.
A brisk and mellow gust of wind.
It goes away.
Silence.
Quiet.

You find it strange.
Why is this wind coming and going, intermittently?
Windows are shut.
Doors are closed.

You realize what it is.

Letters to the Forgotten:

Breath.
You are breathing.
You don't ever notice it, but you are breathing.
You spend all this time wondering why you struggle to love yourself.

But you already do.
If you didn't, you would not still be alive.
If you did not have self-love and self-care, you would not be breathing.

You already have self-love.
You already know what your mind and your body needs, even without the help of anyone else.
Your body is intrinsically capable of self-care.
It is your mind that you let become polluted by the toxicity and chaos around you.

You are told that you must achieve self-love the same way as everyone else.
You are told that you must climb a specific ladder into transcendence.
But you don't have to.
You are already there.

Write down all the words that are running

Through your head this very moment. Do not think. Just write.

Draw an image that represents how you are feeling this very moment.

Do not think. Just draw.

Letters To Me

As part of your own self-love journey, here are some prompts to write your own letters of hope, what you wish to accomplish and feel, how you dream to move on from this dread you are currently facing, and channel the inner strength you have to empower yourself.

A Letter To Those Fighting To Survive:

Live, So Others Can Also Live

A Letter To Those Who Struggle To Forgive Themselves:

Seek Forgiveness From Those Who Believe You Deserve Forgiveness

A Letter To Those Who Have Been Rejected:

Those Who Rejected You Only Deprived Themselves

A Letter To Those Who Do Not Believe In Themselves:

Live For Today, And Eventually You Will

A Letter To Those Who Find It Difficult To Speak Up:

Be The Courageous Ones Who Stand Up For Those Who Cannot

A Letter To Those Who Need A Supportive Hand:

I Am Here, And I Am Not Going Anywhere

Epilogue

Reminder To Love Everyone

T̲h̲e̲ ̲o̲n̲e̲s̲ who hold the biggest smiles are not always the ones who are happiest.

The ones who yell out the biggest cries are not always the ones in need of help.

The ones who seem to have it all together are not always the most successful.

. . .

Letters to the Forgotten:

The ones who say the most words are not always the most intelligent.

The ones with the most hope are not always the most courageous.

The last souls standing are not always the strongest.

Everyone has their own struggles, their own strengths, and their own demons.

Just because someone seems like they are fine, does not necessarily mean that they are.

Just because someone is not outwardly struggling as much as others, does not mean that they are not struggling internally.

We never know how our words and our actions affect others because the faces they show on the outside are not always the ones they feel on the inside.

We all have darkness in our corners, and we all have faces and secrets that we hide from others.

If the person next to you seems happier than you do, do not assume that they are not sad.

If the person next to you seems miserable, do not assume that they do not have hope and a fighting chance at life.

Be the person who learns to read people by interacting with them and learning about who they really are rather than predicting how they are based on their appearances.

. . .

Your happy-go-lucky neighbor can very well be struggling with depression while you are too busy focusing on those crying for help.

Do not assume.
    Listen.
    Open your heart to everyone.

Reminder To Love Everyone

The ones who hold the biggest smiles are not always the ones who are happiest.
The ones who yell out the biggest cries are not always the ones in need of help.
The ones who seem to have it all together are not always the most successful.

The ones who say the most words are not always the most intelligent.
The ones with the most hope are not always the most courageous.
The last souls standing are not always the strongest.

Everyone has their own struggles, their own strengths, and their own demons.
Just because someone seems like they are fine, does not necessarily mean that they are.

Just because someone is not outwardly struggling as much

Reminder To Love Everyone

as others, does not mean that they are not struggling internally.
We never know how our words and our actions affect others because the faces they show on the outside are not always the ones they feel on the inside.

We all have darkness in our corners, and we all have faces and secrets that we hide from others.
If the person next to you seems happier than you do, do not assume that they are not sad.
If the person next to you seems miserable, do not assume that they do not have hope and a fighting chance at life.

Be the person who learns to read people by interacting with them and learning about who they really are rather than predicting how they are based on their appearances.

Your happy-go-lucky neighbor can very well be struggling with depression while you are too busy focusing on those crying for help.

Do not assume.
Listen.
Open your heart to everyone.

Letters to Those Loved & Lost:

You Will Always Be Remembered

MAD GIRL'S LOVE SONG

I shut my eyes and all the world drops dead;
I lift my lids and all is born again.
(I think I made you up inside my head.)

The stars go waltzing out in blue and red,
and arbitrary blackness gallops in:
I shut my eyes and all the world drops dead.

I dreamed that you bewitched me into bed
and sung me moon-struck, kissed me quite insane.

(I think I made you up inside my head.)

God topples from the sky, hell's fires fade:
exit seraphim and Satan's men:

I shut my eyes and all the world drops dead.

I fancied you'd return the way you said,
but I grow old and I forget your name.

(I think I made you up inside my head.)

I should have loved a thunderbird instead;
at least when spring comes they roar back again.

I shut my eyes and all the world drops dead.
(I think I made you up inside my head.)

- Sylvia Plath

Prologue

Love.

When it is right, it can be a beautiful thing.
However, when it is not, it can create destruction far
beyond our imaginations.
Love can be innocent.

Lena Ma

Love sends shivers down our spines and makes us feel as if we are floating.
Love gives us gifts and comfort, and it makes us never want to let go of the source it is coming from.
However, love can also be deadly.
Love can suck us in and spit us out dry.
Love can become obsessive and evil.

Love can manipulate us into doing unspeakable acts that we feel we cannot control.
Love can force us to become so narrow-minded that nothing and no one else matters.
Love can only be innocent or deadly if we allow it.
Love is an empty vessel.

Love absorbs the energy and emotions we put inside it rather than acting as a force that controls our minds.
Love can be changed.
Love has changed.

Haven't you ever been in romantic relationships, where one minute you feel as if you're floating, and the next, you feel as if you were a puppet?
Haven't you ever been in romantic relationships, where you just wanted to get out, but feel like you cannot?
Haven't you ever been in romantic relationships, where you

Letters to Those Loved & Lost:

turn from being madly in love to having complete resentment toward your partner?
This is what love does to us.

Love is so overpowering and so overwhelming that it makes us doubt and resent even ourselves.
Love can change the way we see ourselves and the world so drastically that sometimes we cannot revert.
Love makes us see the world differently depending on which side we are on.

Love makes us feel as if we are being controlled.
Are we though?

Chapter One

**A Letter To My First Crush:
You Are The Reason I Am Capable Of Love**

I am a young girl.
Six.
Shy.
Afraid.
Unlovable.

Lena Ma

Then I see you.
You are perfect.
Everyone loves you.
I love you.
But you don't notice me.

Then one day, that all changes.
When you turn my life around.
You give me a card.
Teddy bears.
Hugging.
In love.
Like you and me.
The card means you love me back.
Right?

I wait.
And wait.
And wait.
And wait.
For eight years.
You pretend like you do not notice me.
Was the card meant for someone else?

Was the card just a card?
Do you even know who I am?
Do you even know my name?
Do you see the way I look at you?

Day after day, I see other girls flirting with you.
Year after year, I watch you date my friends and enemies
while leaving me behind.

Letters to Those Loved & Lost:

Do you not notice how I always make an effort to sit next to you?
Do you not notice how I treat you above everyone else?

To me, that card made me find love.
To you, that card was just a cheap card you gave to everyone.
I found love.
You are my first love.
You are my imaginary love.

Write a letter expressing your true feelings to your first crush.

What do you wish you could do differently? Do not suppress. Just write.

Draw an image representing the agony of how you feel around your first crush.

Do not suppress. Just draw.

Chapter Two

**A Letter To The One Who Keeps Fucking With My Head:
You Are The Reason I Have Self-Doubt**

I see the way you look at me.
Always peeking toward my direction and hinting to

Letters to Those Loved & Lost:

hang out.
I see you.
But it's okay.
Because I like you too.

You message me funny memes, hoping they will make me smile.
They don't.
But I smile anyway.
Just for you.

I flirt with you.
You flirt back.
I flirt with you again.
You ignore me.
Wait.
What?

I don't hear from you for five days.
Then I get another meme.
I smile.
I flirt with you again.
You flirt back.
Then you leave again.
Leaving me confused.
Wondering if you ever liked me.
Or if this is all a lie.

Lena Ma

I see you look at me one minute.
Then I see you look at someone else the next.
Are you fucking with me?
Are you playing with my head?
Back and forth.
Back and forth.
Back and forth.

You continue to mess with my mind.
I'm sorry.
I have to call it quits.
I have to block you.
I don't know what your game is, but I have to go.

Maybe I am just delusional.
Maybe you don't actually like me.
Maybe I am just being a fool.
Maybe you don't like me after all.
I'm sorry.
I have to go.

Write a letter expressing your true feelings to your first crush.

What do you wish you could do differently? Do not suppress. Just write.

Draw an image representing the agony of how you feel around your first crush.

Do not suppress. Just draw.

Chapter Three

**A Letter To The Love I Made Up Out Of Loneliness:
You Are The Reason I Am Fucked Up**

You are my first kiss.
My first boyfriend.

Letters to Those Loved & Lost:

My first lover.
You love me for me.

You are always around when I need you.
You stroke my hair.
You caress me.
You tell me everything will be okay as you sleep next to me at night.

Every night you remind me that I am special.
Every night you remind me that I am loved.
Every night you promise me you will never leave.
Every night you tell me you love me.

But then one day.
You disappear.
And you never come back.
Where are you?
What the hell happened?
Do you not love me anymore?
What happened to the promises you made?
I love you!
Fuck you!

Night after night, I do not hear from you.

Lena Ma

Night after night, I cry myself to sleep.
Night after night, I wonder where you are or who you are with.
Night after night, I caress myself.
Night after night, I fall apart.

Then one night, I turn thirteen.
And I realize something.
You are not real.
You were never real.
You were only my imagination.
Created to help me cope with loneliness.
I fell in love with you when I thought I had no one.

I fell in love with you to help me deal with life.
And now you are gone.
But you will always be in my memories.
I love you.
Forever.
And ever.

Write a letter expressing your true feelings to your first crush.

What do you wish you could do differently? Do not suppress. Just write.

Draw an image representing the agony of how you feel around your first crush.

Do not suppress. Just draw.

Chapter Four

**A Letter To The One I Rejected And Regretted:
You Are The Reason I Am Self-Destructive**

You're always there.
A timid and quiet young boy.
Who always seemed like he didn't belong.

Letters to Those Loved & Lost:

I don't really speak to you.
I don't really notice you.
You are just kind of...there.

Then one day, you reach out.
You express your feelings for me.
I laugh in your face.
I spit in your face.
My first real potential for love, and I laugh instead.
You attempt to ask me out several more times.
Time after time, I respond with distasteful humor and discontent.

You move on.
You find someone else.
You fall in love.

Two years later, I fall in love with you.
Karma's a bitch.
You are already with someone else.
You reject me.
You laugh in my face.
You spit in my face.
Karma, right?

Lena Ma

You try being my friend.
You try not to hurt me.
But because you are with someone, that meant I do not have a place in your life or your heart.
You force yourself to detach from me.

You leave.
You come back because you don't want to actually leave.
But you get in trouble.
So, you leave again.
Each time, I fall apart.
I break.
I crumble.

I lose myself.
I fall into a pattern of self-destruction because I cannot handle unrequited love.
Karma is a bitch.
Right?

Write a letter expressing your true feelings to your first crush.

What do you wish you could do differently? Do not suppress. Just write.

Draw an image representing the agony of how you feel around your first crush.

Do not suppress. Just draw.

Chapter Five

**A Letter To The Hand Who Slaps Me Across The Face:
You Are The Reason I Run From My Past**

I have nothing left.
No school. No job. Just food and regret.

Letters to Those Loved & Lost:

Vomiting. Cutting. Hating.
I feel alone.

I feel unloved.
I feel broken and defective.
I try online dating.
To distract myself from the enemy that is my mind.
I meet you.
You are charming.
You show interest in me.
You distract me from my problems.
I fall head over heels.

We talk every day.
You treat me with respect, and you help me figure out my life.
I am grateful for you.
Then you disappear.
We fade away.
We lose touch.

I never forget about you.
I always think about you whenever I feel down.
You are my angel.
You are my hand.

Lena Ma

Five years later, we meet again.
However, this time it feels different.
You no longer act as my angel.
You no longer behave as my hand.
You are now judgmental and cold.
You now hurt me more than you help me.

You are not who I thought you were five years ago.
We felt so connected then.
So in tune.
I believed that I could count on you.

Then I meet you in person.
And all you want to do is hurt me and judge my character.
Maybe we lost touch for a reason.
Maybe we were never meant to reconnect.
This is goodbye again.
This time for real.

Write a letter expressing your true feelings to your first crush.

What do you wish you could do differently? Do not suppress. Just write.

Draw an image representing the agony of how you feel around your first crush.

Do not suppress. Just draw.

Chapter Six

**A Letter To My First Intimate Love:
You Are The Reason I Possess Anger And Rage**

The first few months with you feels amazing.
You keep me away from my toxic behaviors.
You treat me like a princess.

Letters to Those Loved & Lost:

You give me everything I could possibly want.
And you never complain.
The only thing you cannot do is be honest with me.

Until it is too late.
I hear my phone go off.
And there you are.
With one of your many text messages.
This time, in the form of a break-up.
Break-up via text?
Really?

I try calling you.
You ignore me.
I continue to call you, nonstop, over the next six hours.
Your only response is another text saying we are over at hour five.

I become devastated.
I go for a walk in the park at night and cry in front of strangers.
I try and distract myself with movies only to find myself texting you.
Of all the men I have known so far, you are my first.

Lena Ma

We started off as partners, lovers, confidants, fiancés.
Then we became enemies.
You broke my heart and sent me to be locked away.
Against my will.
Complete shutdown.
I can never forgive you.

Even when you do come back begging for forgiveness.
I no longer see you in the light I used to.
The promises we have made to each other and the love we have felt for each other no longer exist.
I do not love you anymore.

Stop calling me.
Leave me alone.
I'm done.
Asshole.

Write a letter expressing your true feelings to your first crush.

What do you wish you could do differently? Do not suppress. Just write.

Draw an image representing the agony of how you feel around your first crush.

Do not suppress. Just draw.

Chapter Seven

A Letter To The One I Meet Under Lockdown: You Are The Reason I Am No Longer Logical

I meet you in the last place I would ever want to meet someone.

Letters to Those Loved & Lost:

In a psychiatric hospital.
I do not want to associate with anyone, but you force yourself into my life.
You take advantage of my vulnerable side and I fall in love with you.

We spend nights walking around the ward, talking about philosophy and our future together.
You lock me in.
I discharge in bliss.

Three weeks later, you send me a letter.
A letter expressing your love for me and how you want me to be your girlfriend.
I am excited.
I hold onto this letter.
I reach out to give you my answer.
But you do not respond.

I write a letter back and put it in your mailbox.
Yes, I stalk you.
And I find you.
You do not answer.

Lena Ma

Days go by.
Weeks go by.
Months go by.
You reach out and ask me to meet you at a hotel.
It is clear you are trying to keep me a secret.
But I go along with it anyway.
Foolishly.

I meet up with you, and you leave soon after.
After having gotten what you came for.
You ignore me again, using your medication as an excuse.
I fall for it.

Days go by.
Weeks go by.
Months go by.
You reach out again.

I am excited.
You tell me you have met someone and are in a serious relationship.
Why would you tell me that?
Why would I want to hear that?
Why would I care?

Letters to Those Loved & Lost:

Days go by.
Weeks go by.
Months go by.
Silence.

Write a letter expressing your true feelings to your first crush.

What do you wish you could do differently? Do not suppress. Just write.

Draw an image representing the agony of how you feel around your first crush.

Do not suppress. Just draw.

Chapter Eight

A Letter To The One Who Takes Advantage Of Me:
You Are The Reason I Remain Silent

My roommate said you raped me.
Did you?

Letters to Those Loved & Lost:

I know we went out.
I know you bought me drinks.
Did you drug them?
What did you do to them?

What did you do to me?
I thought we were having a fun and casual date.
You show me your favorite bars, handing me drinks as I am distracted.
I should have known better.
But I am greedy for free cocktails, and I go along with it.

You introduce me to your friends and acquaintances,
handing me drinks sporadically, as I sip on them, distracted.
Eight drinks later, I am in the bathroom, vomiting.
Crying.
Near death.

I quietly whisper, "I need help", but no one hears me.
I know, while throwing up, that you are trouble.
However, no one notices.
No one realizes I am in pain and danger.
Everyone assumes that I am another drunk college student.
Not a victim.

Lena Ma

I get a cab.
You climb in with me.
No.
Get out.
But I am too weak and drunk to tell you so.

We go back to my dorm.
You put me in bed.
Tuck me in.
And instead of leaving, you climb in with me.
You undress me.
One item at a time.
Take advantage of me.

Hold my hair while I puke but continue to feel around.
Am I conscious?
Am I agreeing to this?
Am I giving you signs that I want this?
Was my roommate, right?
Did you rape me?

Write a letter expressing your true feelings to your first crush.

What do you wish you could do differently? Do not suppress. Just write.

Draw an image representing the agony of how you feel around your first crush.

Do not suppress. Just draw.

Chapter Nine

**A Letter To My Longest, Yet Most Toxic, Relationship:
You Are The Reason I Am Traumatized**

You show up at my house, flowers in hand, charming as ever.

Letters to Those Loved & Lost:

I am still in pain, so I fall for you immediately.
To this day, I still do not know whether I loved you.
We have an amazing first date and an amazing connection.
I want more.

I take two-hour bus rides to your apartment, a four-hour roundtrip.
I do not mind.
Then the fights begin.
One month into the relationship.

We argue, and you kick me out of your apartment, forcing me to stand outside in the dark, waiting for the next bus.
We fight, and you run off to other women for your emotional comfort instead of talking to me.
We both know our love is dysfunctional.
But we brush it off.

We pretend our toxic fights never happen.
And we love each other again.
For a week.
Then the cycle continues.

We love. We fight. We love again.
I then move in with you.

Lena Ma

Six months in.
Against my better judgment.

We argue again, and you force me to move out.
I move into my own apartment.
I give you a call.
You say you still love me.
We get back together.

The cycle continues.
We love. We fight. We love again.
You then move in with me.
Against my better judgment.
We fight, and you move in with another woman.

I call you again.
You say you still love me.
We rent an apartment together and the fights get worse.
You hit me.
You refuse to pay rent.
You blame me for you losing your job.
What did I do?

Why am I still in this toxic relationship?

Letters to Those Loved & Lost:

A toxic relationship consumed by physical abuse and
infidelity.
I try leaving.
But I can't.
You move out.

I convince you to move back in.
Against my better judgment.
The cycle continues.
We love. We fight. We love again.

Then you ignore me.
Screaming at me for moving around in my own apartment.
You leave again.

This time I learn.
I stop calling.
I stop caring.
I stop loving.
You are my most toxic relationship.
And I am never going back.

Write a letter expressing your true feelings to your first crush.

What do you wish you could do differently? Do not suppress. Just write.

Draw an image representing the agony of how you feel around your first crush.

Do not suppress. Just draw.

Chapter Ten

**A Letter To The Unexpected And Shallow Breakup:
You Are The Reason I Despise Men**

You are perfect.

Letters to Those Loved & Lost:

In your fashionable suits and your stylish hats.
You laugh at all my jokes.
You listen to all my problems.
As inappropriate as they are.

We spend hours talking on the phone.
Our longest record is six.
I think.
I can't remember.
That's the longest time I have ever spoken to anyone.

You compliment me, and you seem genuinely happy to be with me.
But that is a lie.
Isn't it?

You never return my hints to take the relationship further.
You still talk to other women in hopes for a potential long-term partner.
I am not good enough.
Never for you.
Why are you with me then?
Why do you still come over if you do not see a future with me?

Lena Ma

Then you call me up.
One month later.
You tell me it is over and that you have had doubts since week one.
The first week?
What the hell were you doing during the other three weeks?

We talk on the phone.
For hours.
You tell me I'm inconvenient.
I live less than an hour from you.
I cry in the middle of the street.

You only stay for as long as you do because you do not want to upset me.
Then you hang up.
And I am still in shock.
I smash all the gifts you have given me.
I regret opening my heart to you only to have it crushed so soon.

Our relationship seemed fine.
Perfect even.
Now it is over.
Just as quickly as it began.
You are the reason I begin writing.

Letters to Those Loved & Lost:

So thank you.
But fuck you.

Two days later, I see pictures of you with someone else.
Good luck to her.
Fuck her.

Write a letter expressing your true feelings to your first crush.

What do you wish you could do differently? Do not suppress. Just write.

Draw an image representing the agony of how you feel around your first crush.

Do not suppress. Just draw.

Chapter Eleven

**A Letter To The One I Left Unexpectedly:
You Are The Reason I Deserve To Be Ghosted**

You did nothing wrong.
I'm sorry.

Letters to Those Loved & Lost:

You are not at fault.
I am.

I find it difficult letting others down when I am not interested.
That is what I am doing to you.
I'm sorry.
I do not want to spend my life with someone who only talks about Jesus.

I cannot start a relationship with someone who already has kids.
I am shallow.
I know.
I should have been honest with you.
Instead of ghosting you.

I am making the wrong choice.
I turn down and hurt a perfect gentleman when all you want to do is watch a movie.
I still regret it.
I know you do not care.
But I still regret the impulsive actions I have made on my part.

Lena Ma

I'm sorry.
You do not have to forgive me.
I do not expect you to forgive me.
You do not even need to know if I am sorry or not.
I'm just sorry.

Write a letter expressing your true feelings to your first crush.

What do you wish you could do differently? Do not suppress. Just write.

Draw an image representing the agony of how you feel around your first crush.

Do not suppress. Just draw.

Chapter Twelve

**A Letter To The One Who Could Have Been:
You Are The Reason I Have No Standards**

Up until now, I thought I was alone in my witty sarcasm
and terrible humor.
The first day I meet you, you take my breath away.

Letters to Those Loved & Lost:

I feel like I can be myself around you, and I have the best first date of my life.
We connect so well, and sparks shoot everywhere.

However, there is one problem.
Not really.
Before we met, you told me you are not looking for anyone serious.
I choose to ignore that.
I see you as an amazing potential partner, and I do everything I can think of to get you to be with me.

I buy you gifts.
I give you space.
I share my feelings with you more times than I can count.
Every time we meet up, I feel like I never want the night to end.

You are perfect person for me, yet the perfect person I cannot have.
You keep telling me that we are not together.
I keep refusing to believe you.
We have great phone conversations, and you cheer me up every single time.

Lena Ma

The more we talk, the more I see you as a boyfriend.
I ask you if you are dating anyone, and I pretend like I do not want you.
You tell me to mind my own business.
I continue to open my heart to you, sharing personal information and finding excuses to get closer to you.

You realize this.
I know you realize this.
Because you pull away the closer I come.
Every night I dream about you.
Wondering how my future would look with you in it.
I feel complete when I am around you.

When I am with you, there is not one dull moment.
But I am delusional.
You go from texting back once a day to once a week to once every three months.
Radio silence.

Then I see you with another woman.
Clearly in a relationship.
Nothing serious, my ass.

Write a letter expressing your true feelings to your first crush.

What do you wish you could do differently? Do not suppress. Just write.

Draw an image representing the agony of how you feel around your first crush.

Do not suppress. Just draw.

Chapter Thirteen

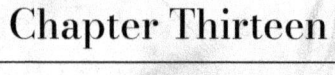

**A Letter To The One Who Fell For All My Bullshit:
You Are The Reason I Have No Shame**

You are a nice person.
A great person.

Letters to Those Loved & Lost:

I know that.
But I treat you like crap anyway.

Truth is, when we first met, I immediately knew I do not want to be with you.
But I continue to see you anyway.
As a distraction.
Out of boredom.

I make you drive over two hours to see me because I am bored.
I know.
I'm sorry.
But I do it again.
And again.

Every time I am bored.
I should have told you I am not interested sooner.
Rather than telling you, I ignore you instead, just like others have ignored me.
I string you along, and you fall for it.
I know.
I'm sorry.
But when I do tell you I am not interested, we argue, we fight, and I feel guilty.

Lena Ma

A couple weeks go by.
I become bored again.
And I need another distraction.
I turn back to you because I know you will answer me.
You do.

We get back together.
I feel uneasy again.
I ignore you.
You realize it.
I continue making excuses to keep you around.

Our relationship always turns me off.
I tell you I am not seeing anyone else, but then I do.
I go back to you when it is convenient.
When I am lonely.

I know you see my flaws.
Yet, you stick around anyway.
While I turn to others.
I know.
I'm sorry.
But I will not change.

Write a letter expressing your true feelings to your first crush.

What do you wish you could do differently? Do not suppress. Just write.

Draw an image representing the agony of how you feel around your first crush.

Do not suppress. Just draw.

Chapter Fourteen

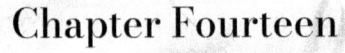

**A Letter To The One Who Refuses To Stop:
You Are The Reason I Fear Others**

I know what you're thinking.
You're thinking that just because I ask you to sit next to me,
it means I want to sleep with you.

Letters to Those Loved & Lost:

No.
I am not.

Stop thinking that.
But that idea is already stuck in your head.
Isn't it?
I know because you invite yourself into my apartment and make your way inside of me.

I know because even when I push you away, you persist and hold me down.
I know because even when I tell you to leave, you continue to forcibly move your hands.
I freeze.
Traumatized.
Hoping the night will just end so I have an excuse to force you to leave.

I cry, and I hate the feeling of you touching me.
I pray this moment ends because I feel disgusting and abused.
I just want you to go.
Please stop.
I beg you.
Just stop.
I don't want to do this.

Lena Ma

Why did I let you in?
Why didn't I call the cops?
Oh god.
Please just stop!

The morning comes.
I cry with joy.
I get up and tell you to leave so I can go to work.
I lock myself in the bathroom for an hour.
I come out.
You're still here.
Smoking a joint when you are clearly inexperienced.

I tell you to leave now.
You resist.
I repeat myself.
This time, louder and angrier.

You finally leave, with hopes that you will see me again.
I do not correct you.
You text me hours later.
I block you.

Write a letter expressing your true feelings to your first crush.

What do you wish you could do differently? Do not suppress. Just write.

Draw an image representing the agony of how you feel around your first crush.

Do not suppress. Just draw.

Chapter Fifteen

**A Letter To The One Who Ghosted Me:
I Deserve It.
Karma Does Exist.**

You saw my crazy early on.
Or at least, the lower spectrum of it.

Letters to Those Loved & Lost:

You are one of those people.
What do you call them?
The "ghosters".

I knew you did not like me after the way our first date ended.
Why don't you just tell me?
Instead of making me reach out to you.
Coming off as insane and crazy.

I really tried with you.
I quell my crazy behaviors, and I wait for you, patiently.
However, you continue to ignore me.
Using the excuse that you do not have to respond to my texts "immediately".
Texting back "immediately" means within a few seconds.
Not within a few weeks.

I thought we had a great time.
I send you my stories.
I wish you luck on your workshop.
I support your career even though I think it is stupid.
But you still ignore me.

You then let me know that you will reach out "soon".

Lena Ma

I get my hopes up.
That was nine months ago.
What is your definition of "soon"?
Good luck with your acting career.
You are a great liar.

Write a letter expressing your true feelings to your first crush.

What do you wish you could do differently? Do not suppress. Just write.

Draw an image representing the agony of how you feel around your first crush.

Do not suppress. Just draw.

Chapter Sixteen

**A Letter To The One Who Calls Me A Freak For Being Myself:
You Are The Reason I Pretend To Be Someone I'm Not**

Letters to Those Loved & Lost:

I meet up with you.
You're nothing special.
Just someone I needed to distract myself from my problems.
I do not need you.

But you don't know that.
I need you to need me.
But not the other way around.

We go out.
I don't know what I'm doing.
I just pretend I do.
To impress you.
Why?

I have no idea.
I just want you to stick around.
I don't even like you.
But you don't know that.

We come back.
I thought the date went horribly.
I still don't like you.
But you don't know that.
You still seem to like me.

Lena Ma

So, I just go with it.

You make a move.
I still don't like you.
But I do not stop you.
I let it go.
I miss the attention.
I crave human touch.

I become vulnerable even when my feelings are only disgust.
I let it go.
I get my attention.
You get what you want.
You get off.
And then you leave.

The next morning, you become angry that I had made plans that do not involve you.
You hate that I do not put you first.
You hate that you are not getting what you want all the time.

You become resentful.
You manifest your anger onto me.

Letters to Those Loved & Lost:

You call me a "freak", as well as many other insults.

You end the conversation by blocking me before I even have the chance to look at my phone.
I brush it off.
I don't care.
I don't like you.
I never liked you.
But you will never know that.

Write a letter expressing your true feelings to the one you open up to because you crave love and attention. What do you wish you could do differently? Do not suppress. Just write.

Write a letter expressing your true feelings to your first crush.

What do you wish you could do differently? Do not suppress. Just write.

Draw an image representing the agony of how you feel around your first crush.

Do not suppress. Just draw.

Chapter Seventeen

**A Letter To The One Who Lured Me In With No Intention Of Keeping Me:
You Are The Reason I Question My Judgments**

You have everything.
Looks.

Letters to Those Loved & Lost:

Charm.
Humor.
Career.
Life.
While I am still a simpleton looking for love.

You find me lovely.
You find me quirky.
You see me as a potential partner.
Or that's what I thought.
No.

Now I know.
You only saw me as another fling.
To get what you want.
Then to throw me out.

You thought I was stupid.
You thought I was too naïve to know what was going on.
You were right.
I was naïve.
I was so desperate to find love that I could not see the reality of the situation.

We start off innocent.

Lena Ma

Coffee.
Board games.
Music.

Then it becomes awkward.
Then you change.
The monster comes out.
I no longer recognize you.
The person I have known for two days.
Now becomes someone seeking lust, and lust alone.

What happened?
Why did I agree to go along with this?
What is wrong with me?
Why did I travel three hours just to be used?
Then it stops.

You get up.
Escort me out of your apartment.
And I never hear from you again.

Write a letter expressing your true feelings to your first crush.

What do you wish you could do differently? Do not suppress. Just write.

Draw an image representing the agony of how you feel around your first crush.

Do not suppress. Just draw.

Chapter Eighteen

A Letter To The One Who Thinks I Will Never Be Good Enough: You Are The Reason I Turn Against Myself

You're old.
You're ugly.

Letters to Those Loved & Lost:

You're shallow.
I can never see myself with you.
I can never like you.

So, why am I still texting you?
Why am I still sending flirts and images back and forth?
Why am I still letting arguments with you tear me apart?
Why am I still hoping that you will love me?
Why am I still talking to you?

I should have let you go when you first decided to ignore me.
I should have let you go when I knew this isn't going anywhere.
I should have let you go when you first asked me to do things that were against my beliefs.
I should have let you go when I knew I am never going to love you.
I should have let you go when I saw you.

Why did I persist?
Was it because of loneliness?
Was it because I knew you were interested so I tried holding onto that?
Was it because I thought I would regret it if I let you go?
Was it because I thought I couldn't do better?
Was it because I just wanted someone to love me?

Never have I ever felt so controlled by someone I didn't even like.
Never have I ever thought I would surrender everything I am for everything I'm not.
Never have I ever thought I would completely lose myself for a man.
Never have I ever thought I would get out of the mess you had pulled me in.

But I did.
So, take your flirts and your images, and guilt-trip someone else with unwanted solicitations.

Write a letter expressing your true feelings to your first crush.

What do you wish you could do differently? Do not suppress. Just write.

Draw an image representing the agony of how you feel around your first crush.

Do not suppress. Just draw.

Chapter Nineteen

**A Letter To The Love I Have Found:
Will You Leave Too?
Or Will My Pattern Of Unfortunate
Relationships Finally Come To An End?**

Letters to Those Loved & Lost:

When I met you, I had no idea what I wanted.
I almost didn't show up.
I was not at a place where I cared enough to try.

But I show up anyway.
And there you are.
Quiet.
Mysterious.
Different.

The night starts off as the other nights.
Uncomfortable.
New.
Awkward.
Silent.

But then something changes.
As if some power overcame me.
And I share with you everything.
My flaws.
My traumas.
My insecurities.
My past.
And you do not run away.

Lena Ma

Surprising.
That's a first.
Soon, we become closer.
Sharing every part of our lives with each other.
We see each other as potential partners.

You see no faults in me.
You're different.
You stay.
Not out of obligation.
Not out of desperation.
But out of love.

That's different.
That's pressure.
That's scary.

I hope I don't mess it up.
I'll probably mess it up.
My track record.
I'm a mess.

But you hold on.
You stay.
Even when I do mess up.

Letters to Those Loved & Lost:

Is that true love?
Am I capable of true love?

I may never know the answer.
I guess we shall see.
Where our journey takes us.
I guess we shall see.
Whether you end up only in my memories.
I love you.

Write a letter expressing your true feelings to your first crush.

What do you wish you could do differently? Do not suppress. Just write.

Draw an image representing the agony of how you feel around your first crush.

Do not suppress. Just draw.

Chapter Twenty

**A Letter To The Person I Have Neglected My Entire Life:
You Are My One True Love, And I Will Never Leave You Again**

Letters to Those Loved & Lost:

I have pushed you aside my entire life.
Always choosing men and obsessive love over you.
I'm sorry.

I have hurt you and insulted you, in hopes that I would
obtain potential love.
I'm sorry.
I have forced you into situations that have made you cry and
have turned my back on you when all you wanted was
a hug.
I'm sorry.

I have hated you for making me choose and lied to you for
making me wait.
I'm sorry.

I'm sorry for putting you in situations that made you hate
yourself.
I'm sorry for forcing you to go against your beliefs which
have made you hurt yourself.
I'm sorry for all the words I have said when I thought I
meant them.
I'm sorry for always putting you last while my desperation
first.
I'm sorry.

Lena Ma

Will you ever forgive me?
Will you ever let me back in?
Will you ever trust me again?
After all I have put you through?
Will you ever love me again?
Have you ever loved me?

Do I still have a chance?
Or is it time to let go?
Have my actions been so drastic that there is no turning back?
I want to love you again.

I want to be there for you through thick and thin.
I want to never let another boy, or another man, come between you and me.

I want to show you that you do not deserve neglect and hatred, despite how much you were shown before.
I want to show you that you are worthy of being loved.
I want to love you.
Please love me back.

Write a letter expressing your true feelings to your first crush.

What do you wish you could do differently? Do not suppress. Just write.

Draw an image representing the agony of how you feel around your first crush.

Do not suppress. Just draw.

Epilogue

Emotions are powerful.
Emotions make us feel as if we are engaging in actions we cannot control.
Emotions make us impulsively react to situations that we later regret.

Letters to Those Loved & Lost:

Emotions make us become desperate when it comes to finding love and when we are losing love.
Emotions can make us become crazy.
We turn into tears.
We turn into fury.
We turn into resentment, where we are only focused on two things.
Revenge.
And new love.

Our emotions become so strong that, instead of turning inward when a relationship ends, we remain outward.
We jump from potential partner to potential partner because our emotions desperately make us find replacements rather than learn to love ourselves.
We believe we are massively flawed when our love is not returned.

We fail to see that the opinions of others do not define our worth.
And that our opinions of ourselves are the only ones that do.
We need to reframe our emotions and stop using them to define our personalities and actions.
We need to discover who we are outside of unrequited and destructive love, and realize that we do not have to be destroyed by them.

Lena Ma

Can we finally learn that love does not control us after all?
Can we finally learn that love is only defined by the emotions we feed into it?
Or will we perish once again the next time someone buys us a ring and takes it away?
Do not perish.

Love Letter

Not easy to state the change you made.
If I'm alive now, then I was dead,
Though, like a stone, unbothered by it,
Staying put according to habit.
You didn't just tow me an inch, no--
Nor leave me to set my small bald eye
Skyward again, without hope, of course,
Of apprehending blueness, or stars.

That wasn't it. I slept, say: a snake
Masked among black rocks as a black rock
In the white hiatus of winter--
Like my neighbors, taking no pleasure
In the million perfectly-chisled
Cheeks alighting each moment to melt
My cheeks of basalt. They turned to tears,
Angels weeping over dull natures,
But didn't convince me. Those tears froze.
Each dead head had a visor of ice.
And I slept on like a bent finger.

Love Letter

The first thing I was was sheer air
And the locked drops rising in dew

Limpid as spirits. Many stones lay
Dense and expressionless round about.
I didn't know what to make of it.
I shone, mice-scaled, and unfolded
To pour myself out like a fluid
Among bird feet and the stems of plants.
I wasn't fooled. I knew you at once.

Tree and stone glittered, without shadows.
My finger-length grew lucent as glass.
I started to bud like a March twig:
An arm and a leg, and arm, a leg.
From stone to cloud, so I ascended.
Now I resemble a sort of god
Floating through the air in my soul-shift
Pure as a pane of ice. It's a gift.

- Sylvia Plath

An acknowledgment to all my past relationships and potential loves. I hope one day you are also able to escape the perils of your emotions.

The Passion Of My Desolation

Chapter 1

The Blade Of My Right Hand

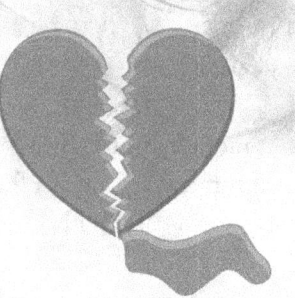

The pain I feel deep inside is like none I have ever experienced before.
The expression of my woes leaves me speechless and cold.
My heart is dead; my blood runs still; my soul always yearning for more,
Even as the days pass me, my eyes cry for you as I turn old.

Lena Ma

They say time heals all wounds, and your betrayal will soon be forgotten,
What they don't realize is how swiftly you came into my life, like a sweet, summer breeze,
Allowing me to trust you, love you, believe in you, now leaving my memories rotten.
I opened myself to you, vulnerable, and you brought me to my knees.

I thought you were different; I thought you were real.
You pushed me to the ground, left me in tears for what you have done.
I thought you were perfect, the way you made me feel,
And I knew I had to leave, but you took away my courage to run.

You stabbed me with a knife and betrayed me when I was down.
I lie awake at night, haunted by our endless fights,
Memories of you suffocating me as I feel ready to drown.
With you gone, I can finally enter the light.

We were so close, so connected, never knowing what we may find.
I knew they changed you, tampering your brain, turning you corrupt.
The others who came and went wounded my body, but you wounded my mind.
Times are different now; I'm ready to give up.

I can still hear your voice; the stillness inside me will never fade away.

The Passion Of My Desolation

You tell me we will never be the same as you watch me burn up in flames.
I cry for help; I cry for you, knowing you will never stay.
I blame myself, while you stand there holding onto my shame.

I miss you, my friend, goodbye forever as I feel myself nearing death.
With this blade I forgive you, as I take my final breath.

Chapter 2

My Heart, I Surrender

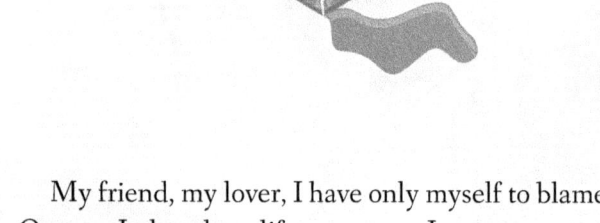

My friend, my lover, I have only myself to blame.
On you, I placed my life, your trust I can never amend.
You hear me call for you, my hand reaching out, screaming your name,
But you ignore me, turning away, like it was all pretend.

I can clearly remember the day we met,
Your hair golden brown, and your eyes ocean blue.

The Passion Of My Desolation

I never met someone so different, placing my life in you like a gambler's bet.
I was so naïve; I loved you, but I didn't have a clue.

But now times are changing, life moving on like you never cared.
You were always by my side, wiping the sadness away from my eyes.
The infidelity, the lies, the deceit, leaving me alone and scared,
Tightly holding onto the little we had as our knot unties.

As I drown inside this bottle, I drink away my sorrows.
I've watched many come and go; I thought, indeed, you were the one.
It doesn't matter anymore, for I know there's no tomorrow.
There's no turning back now as I am finally done.

What happened to us? I will always wonder.
Your wish I grant you; you are now released.
I hear the thunder now, pouring down as I finally surrender,
I hope you live your life; I hope you find peace.

Chapter 3

Terminal Faith

My faith is lost; I cannot hide.
My heart locked in a cage, my mind splashing with rage; I wish I could heal.
My time is near, no time for fear; I know I've tried.
My life feels different now, everything so surreal.

Trying to withhold my fears, I wonder how I got here,

The Passion Of My Desolation

Screaming into my mirror, no longer recognizing the face staring back.
It's consuming my body; each day, a part of me disappears.
My life used to be perfect, but now all I see is black.

This illness changed me into someone I never thought I'd be,
Though I can't complain too much, as I know others are equally in pain.
Locked up in my caged thoughts, despising the days I used to be free.
I can't continue this fight; my blood continues to drain.

I used to be so carefree, now, questioning the meaning of life.
Regretting the moments I took for granted, choices and decisions I had made.
Many mistakes, numerous enemies, all ending in strife,
Moments I've spent in pride and hatred when I should have been afraid.

My time is ending, my family crying as I lie here no longer with faith.
My heart cold as ice, with endless pain that no one can measure.
I'm dying, I tell myself, my mind spinning with wraith,
Leaving the world I lived in, the one that gave me so much pleasure.

Chapter 4

My Last Journey, Forever

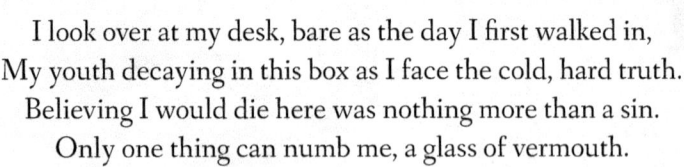

I look over at my desk, bare as the day I first walked in,
My youth decaying in this box as I face the cold, hard truth.
Believing I would die here was nothing more than a sin.
Only one thing can numb me, a glass of vermouth.

I was so innocent, so excited, the day I was hired,
Devoting my entire life, watching all the rest slowly slip away,

The Passion Of My Desolation

Never really expecting the day I might be fired.
The struggles were real, now regretting all the years I decided to stay.

I watched others come and go as I continued to climb the peak,
Secretly lavishing in all the moments when others slipped.
I thought I was special; I thought I was unique,
Karma hitting hard when I finally lost my grip.

The sun continues to descend, my life now turning grey,
If only it wasn't too late to take back all that I have lost.
We don't admit it, but everyone eventually falls to prey.
No longer can I turn back, revisit all the roads I have crossed.

My heart yearns for adventure, but my body has become too frail.
My quest for happiness now much too rare, my shadows suffering in despair.
Walking through the darkness, knowing I can never prevail,
Removing myself from those I've disappointed; my life in solitaire.

I stumble across the tracks, the train heading towards me as I wave my last goodbye.
I hop on, ready to leave this life behind as fate takes my body away.
My life has been nothing but a waste, that I cannot deny.
Whatever happens, I am ready to decay.

Chapter 5

Without You, I Feel Nothing

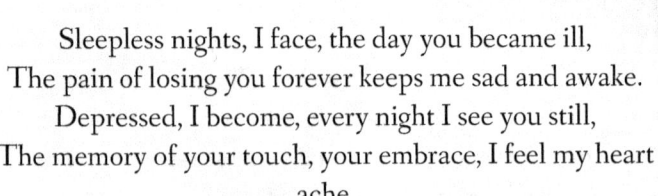

Sleepless nights, I face, the day you became ill,
The pain of losing you forever keeps me sad and awake.
Depressed, I become, every night I see you still,
The memory of your touch, your embrace, I feel my heart ache.

I wish I could hug you, kiss you, heal all your pain.
I would do anything, everything, just to hear your voice.

The Passion Of My Desolation

I wish I could stop the horror coursing through your veins,
If only times were different, if only you had a choice.

Memories of my childhood, I hold onto so dear.
I can still feel the skin of your hand against the skin of mine.
Mother, I miss you, I wish you were here.
You will forever be my Savior, my angel, my divine.

Every night I look for you among the falling stars.
I can no longer face society without fighting back my tears.
I try so hard, but nothing can hide away my scars.
I can never bring you back, but you'll always be in my prayers.

You told me to never suffer, and now I feel ashamed.
Whatever happened to the days when I was simply just afraid?
It's time for me to go, just like I came, unnamed.
I took you for granted, my best friend, I betrayed.
The Comfort Of My Piercing Needle

You made me trust you, believe you were my remedy.
You loved me dearly as I let you embrace my veins.
I thought I would be cool, develop a better identity,
Instead, you destroyed me, your breath worse than cocaine.

I need to get out, leave, scared of what I'll say,
When I lie to those I love, blind to who I see in my mirror.
But every time I run, you always convince me to stay,
For without you with me, I become angry and bitter.

Who have I become? What have I turned into?
It hurts so much, the scars no one can see.

Lena Ma

How did I become so dependent, helpless, hopeless, without you?
I feel so lost, so broken, someone please help me.

You made me your slave, ravished my body and drove me insane.
Every night I slumber alone, you haunt my sleep and come knocking.
Too late for regrets and sorrow, the days I shall never regain.
Nothing surprises me anymore, nothing I find shocking.

My hands cold, my heart blackens, I've become sick of relapsing.
Even as I gasp, no one will aid my pleading cries.
My eyes burn deep; why does this keep happening?
No one to my rescue, all stuck between my truth and lies.

I'm all alone now, waiting for my end.
I used to have it all, trophies and certificates on my shelf.
This piercing needle and glass, now my only friends.
Who am I? I no longer know. End my life as I kill myself.

Chapter 6
Blood Seeps In My Silent Battle

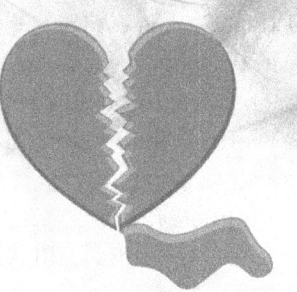

Am I good enough yet for the perfection that you desire?
Starving myself days on end so one day I'll be worthy.
I know I've gone too far, the consequences soon be dire,
But self-hate and pain come second to feeling pretty.

This vicious cycle plagues my mind, sharp misery and blind.
The angry demon chasing me as I reach for perfection.

Lena Ma

Never letting go, even as my health declines.
I can no longer look at myself, repulsed at my reflection.

Another pound is much more than I can ever bear.
I push others away so I can let no one else down.
My claws digging into my skin, every regret forming a tear,
I refuse to cease my silent battle until I fit into my gown.

I can feel the sickness in my blood, struggling to escape.
They lock me up, everyone gone, I pushed them all away.
Cracked lips and tired eyes forming so I can stay in shape,
Lying in this cell alone, my mind my body obeys.

Just be strong, I tell myself, as I lift the fork to my mouth.
Fear and anxiety seep down my hand, tears flowing from my eyes.
"Don't do it," it whispers, a voice I cannot live without.
I place it back down, for tomorrow, I will not rise.

A World Where I Don't Belong

A child born humble into an ever-changing world,
Yet all I see are people, apartheid still grasped strong across their minds.
My ethnicity and skin still course on every page curled,
I thought times had changed, everyone matured, but maybe we're all just blind.

You call it harmless, but my heart throbs with each passing comment.
Exposing me as a flaw, a degenerate, a life deserved to end.
Split between my own image and yours as I'm overwhelmed with lament,
We're all the same, yet on you, my life depends.

The Passion Of My Desolation

Human crudeness at its finest; ignorance surely is bliss.
Judge me by my skin, accusing me without a brain.
Intolerance is acceptable, only on your terms we cannot dismiss.
We're all equally insecure; that's why we place the blame.

We have come too far to live life in this segregation.
Fighting too hard to live in a world free from contention.
We never change, from generation to generation,
Isolating others and tearing them down, all just for attention.

The Queen Behind The Screen

I hate you, but I can never say it to your face.
Rather, leaving open wounds on a page for others to stab.
I find joy in this heartless game I'm trying to chase,
Picking and picking until I'm no longer a scab.

I know you're hurting, crying on the other side.
But I can't stop, finding strength in the numbness I possess.
You've approached me, confronted me, but I've denied,
That I, your best friend, ruining your life, I obsess.

I find peace in my offensive words, gaining attention with each hateful post.
Others say I'm inspiring, living out my best dreams.
You think I'm conniving, but it's really me who I hate the most.
My smile hidden deeper inside, far beneath my screams.

I hear the words I call you, "ugly", "fat", but at least you know who you really are.

Lena Ma

Your resilience as you endure each hateful word makes you that much stronger.
I judge because I know I can never be, never go far,
That's why I sit alone, in the dark, a true, miserable loner.

You try to manage your pain and agony, but at least yours are genuine.
You cry, and you hate, but at least you're aware it's all fake,
While I establish my place hidden on the Internet like a true denizen,
Living a lie behind a screen, unaware if I'm asleep or awake.

Chapter 7

A Robotic Slave

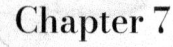

"Stay humble, grow up rich," they always said to me.
Chase the dream of nine to five; you'll never have to worry.
For several decades, I listened, unable to breathe.
I should never have obeyed; here is my story.

This delusion I'm stuck in, with constant worries of whether I'll make it.
I'm drowning in the hands of debt, never being released,

Lena Ma

Trying to fight against it for crimes I did commit,
Forever trapped and surrounded, until I become deceased.

I never wanted my life to end this way.
It started off so innocent, the simple things I bought.
My life crumbling down soon after I could not pay,
The hell I'm in, from a small hole, I thought.

I thought I had it all, the filthy rich holding all the land,
Before becoming a slave to the system with no way out.
If only I had stayed humble and lived life like I planned,
I wouldn't be burying my grave, just to reach for clout.

Chapter 8

Chasing Wind

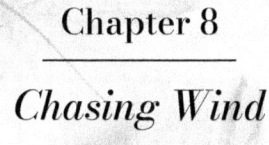

I walk alone deep into the forest, the quiet wind blowing through the trees.
My thoughts begin to slow, my mind entering a deep sleep.
My heart beats slowly as I fall down to my knees,
My emotions running wild, my eyes beginning to weep.

My entire life I spent chasing after my dreams,
Trying so hard to be part of the shallow crowd,

Lena Ma

Just to find out that no one is who they seem.
Now, I walk alone on a floating cloud.

Why do I always chase the love that can never be?
Struggling to find my way back when I fall through the cracks,
Leaving me stranded in the deep ocean sea,
Always leaving myself vulnerable to get stabbed in the back.

I've always dreamt of someone who can take me by the hand,
But instead, I find myself completely empty inside.
The more I scream for attention, the less they understand.
I've lived my whole life as a lie so no one can see I've tried.

Nothing matters anymore; all will be lost when my life soon ends.
My thoughts so overwhelming that I can't even explain.
I'm done trying, no longer will I need to pretend,
As I leave the world the same I entered, my body remains.
Seize The Darkness, End The Light

My soul has been destroyed from the misery I feel,
My life becoming depressed with no meaning left behind.
I live in a world of oppression with nothing that can heal,
If only everyone wasn't so naïve, wasn't so blind.

Feelings of dismay lie deep inside my body; memories washed away.
My thoughts begin to swirl as I cry, darkness seizing the light.
The emotions are too intense, yet they tell me to seize the day,

The Passion Of My Desolation

No matter how hard I've tried, I will always lose the fight.

From endless pain to dark depression, my tears fill with sorrow,
Drowning deeper and deeper with no one to my avail.
No longer do I seize onto hope, waiting for a better tomorrow,
Darkness has consumed me, minimal light remains.

My days of struggle have only left me insane,
The ridicule and torture drive away my will to fight.
I used to be proud, living solely in vain,
Now I'm wasting away, hellfire into the night.

Chapter 9

Survival Of Endless Nights

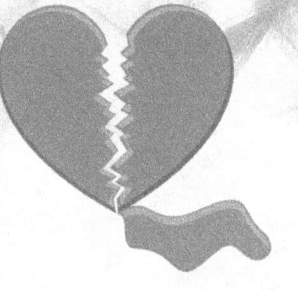

Crippling paralysis, silent screams, when will this nightmare end?
Panic worries and darkness surrounds, smiles plastered on my face.
My mind so afraid, my body so numb, I can only pretend,
That I'm just like you despite praying for God's saving grace.

The Passion Of My Desolation

Not a day passes by without internal fights and endless nights.
My heart compresses, and I find myself unable to breathe.
Feeling like the world has turned against me, leaving me in fright,
Leaving me trembling and shaking on my knees.

This isn't my body; someone please find me.
This feels so unreal, so alone, so unfair.
Fear is the enemy, please just set me free,
These constant battles inside me leaving me impaired.

I cannot leave my home, cannot function in society.
Even the thought of stepping out makes it hard for me to swallow.
No one can understand, inside my mind the ferocity,
I lie awake restless, night after night, hoping for a better tomorrow.

Disappearance At Conception

A lonely child, desperate for attention,
Crying out for mom and dad, just to remain ignored.
Being around them just overwhelms me with tension,
Locked up and barred, my life unexplored.

I shall never know the damage I have done,
The horrors they blame me for, which I cannot even understand.
I wish I could take it back, the words that left me shunned,
Living in this household, forgotten and under fire, is too much to withstand.

Lena Ma

I feel so unwanted, so abandoned, so detached,
Please forgive me, don't lock me behind closed doors.
What have I done, why our bond has become unlatched?
All I ever wanted was a family, to be part of yours.

You ridicule when I cry; you mock when I seek aid,
Never noticing the insanity you have all driven me into.
You played me like a fool; I feel so betrayed,
I'm just a scared child, with absolutely no one to turn to.

Chapter 10

Lady Misfortune

I cannot get up today, my body shivering beneath the sheets,
Face buried in my pillow, sweat pouring down my face.
I'm terrified of this existence, every night it repeats,
To my species, I am nothing but a disgrace.

Is it life that I fear or maybe just my own shadow?
Is it the mistakes I have made or simply the ones I foresee?

Lena Ma

I wish my thoughts didn't lie so deep; I wish they weren't so hollow,
I wish I could just forget; my soul please set me free.

The misfortune of this world will soon come to an end,
All the tragedies in my life will set sail with the passing wind.
I've wasted my life under these sheets, hoping my mind would transcend,
Now it's all gone, ending before it can even begin.

Why do I dread the woes I cannot even comprehend?
Feeling so anxious that my world would crumble down.
The words "brave" and "courage", I will never understand,
My whole life I've been lost, never to be found.

Chapter 11

Nothing But Scars Left Behind

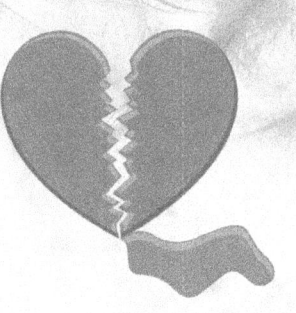

I fade away as the seasons change,
Already regretting the choices I have made.
Every time I speak, I feel so deranged,
As I have accomplished nothing over this past decade.

Who am I without a legacy to leave behind?
Gambling on my own life with never a fighting chance.
They warned me to quit early, to their words I was so blind,

Lena Ma

Now I roam the streets, living in a trance.

I try to change my life, but in its way is my aggression,
Seeking answers only I want to know,
Never realizing that I am falling into deep depression,
Until the day comes where it's time for me to go.

My life has no meaning; I am nothing but a scar,
Placed on this Earth as a blemish.
I thought I could go far; I thought I could become a star,
Instead, I'm left with nothing, from the grounds I will soon perish.

Chapter 12

Stabbing Shadows From My Past

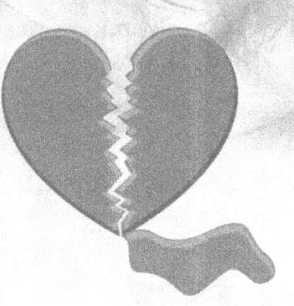

"Stop," I cried, to the flashbacks that still haunt me.
Just a young girl attempting to evade the shadows.
But he didn't stop, continuing to turn the key,
Pressing me down as he promised a better tomorrow.

No one would listen; no one would hear,
Holding in my tears as he continued to pursue,
As I stayed silent, my voice powerless to fear,

Lena Ma

All of these memories I wish I could undo.

I feel so exposed, so broken, my thoughts continue to haunt,
Even as the years pass, the pain continues to overwhelm.
I lie in bed at night, the sheets continuing to taunt,
Like beautiful rose petals, blown from their stems.

The frightened screams and stabbing shadows follow me for decades,
Flashes of teeth and ropes keeping me up at night.
For so long, I've wanted peace, like an end of a soft serenade,
But I feel myself fading, transitioning to a lady in white.

I will never forget him, the one who stole my life,
The one who took away my innocence and left me nothing but rage.
Because of him, I can never find the hope of becoming a wife,
The glee I deserved no longer exists, trapped alone in this tiny cage.

Chapter 13

Individuality Behind The Mask

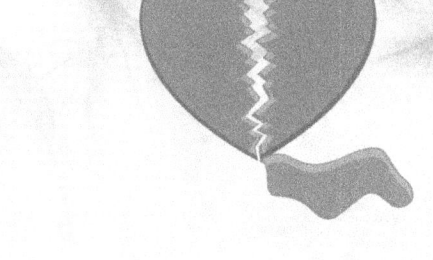

To be part of society requires the relinquishing of your individuality,
Leaving us with this nightmare of darkness and confusion.
I tried so hard to belong that I gave up my personality,
Leaving me with nothing, but delusion and illusion.

Everywhere we look, we see the uprise of more and more clones,

Lena Ma

Until the point where we no longer recognize the person in the mirror.
Similar voices, plastic masks surround, all chilling to the bone,
I hate turning into one of them, but I can see no way clearer.

Conformity has now become the common norm,
Fitting into the standard mold or else live in disarray.
I used to be special, unique, before I transformed,
Now simply trapped behind a shell, my person not on display.

They roam the streets and conquer the Internet,
Unable to distinguish fantasy from reality.
True individuality and substance we all soon forget,
Stuck in this never-ending world of lust and tragedy.

Chapter 14

Tragedy That Is My Existence

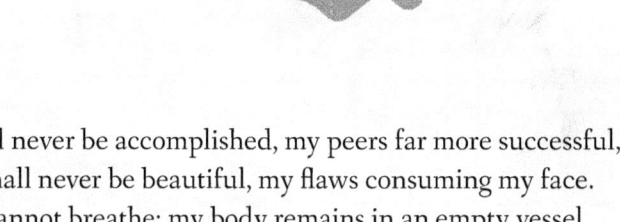

I shall never be accomplished, my peers far more successful,
I shall never be beautiful, my flaws consuming my face.
I cannot breathe; my body remains in an empty vessel,
Of nothingness, my mind and body misplaced.

I want to be like her, confident and glamorous,
Instead, I find in myself loathing and weakness,
Hiding behind shadows so others won't find me cancerous.

Lena Ma

Knowing I'm just different, with definitely no uniqueness.

They ask me how I am, the timid girl sitting in silence.
I respond with positivity, concealing the battle inside my mind.
No one needs to know that behind this smile is pure violence,
Against myself as my mind and body decline.

I hate my existence, just consuming space reserved for others.
I need it to be over, my eyes blinded to the person I perceive.
I am not wanted; no one will ever see my true colors,
If only I had lived a life where I wasn't so naïve.

Chapter 15

Trapped Inside My Treacherous Body

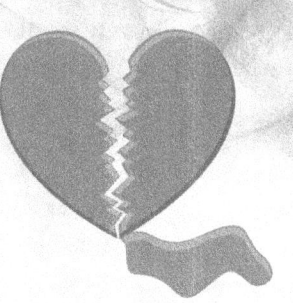

I didn't ask for this; I didn't ask to become a her.
You conceived me without my consent, forcing me to become someone I'm not,
Dressing me up in costumes that make living that much harder,
Disciplining me whenever I'm in something different than what you bought.

Lena Ma

Tradition tells us to conform to one specific gender,
But society has adapted, norms and rules everchanging.
I choose to be who I feel, and I shall not surrender,
Even if I have to fight with all my years remaining.

I hear your judgmental words, disappointed at who I've become,
I'm still your child, caged behind the façade you had me entrapped.
I cannot thrive in this body; I will never succumb,
Accept it or not, but between us, you've created a gap.

Equality does not apply only when they adhere to your standards.
Human rights do not exist only when they favor you.
You have given me life, only to fill it with stander,
Like it or not, to you, I will never be true.

Chapter 16

Lust In My Champagne

The promises you made had me fallen head over heels,
Giving you my heart, foolishly believing you'll keep it safe.
You took me by the hand and told me what we had was real,
Until you left me in the dust, alone in the streets like a waif.

You promised me the world if I'd just give you my body,
You toasted with a ring and the finest bottle of champagne.

Lena Ma

But when those minutes disappeared, you treated me like nobody,
Leaving me for someone else, the love we had in shame.

I still see the imprint of our love around my finger,
Wishing that someday you'll see the error in your ways.
Ten years later, the thoughts of you still linger,
Still holding onto the memory, counting our days.

I still love you, despite knowing the truth,
That you were only with me to satisfy your lust.
I trusted you, allowing you to take away my youth,
Because of you, in no man will I ever trust.

www.ingramcontent.com/pod-product-compliance
Lightning Source LLC
Chambersburg PA
CBHW071956110526
44592CB00012B/1108